a million billion pieces

I once said that *a million billion pieces* was a play about making the time we have count, a concept I didn't give too much thought to when I was the age of this play's characters or the age of the intended audience of middle- and high-schoolers, but it's one I can't get out of my head now. Pria and Theo want to fit everything into the time they believe they have left. When they don't immediately explode (what a short play that would be), it's enough for them to start doubting the mythologies they live by. To challenge the truths we hold about ourselves is no easy task.

Pria and Theo's in-person meeting after a year of "safe" online interactions is their act of defiance against science, rumour, and time. I'm sometimes not sure these two should have ever met, especially when I think of parallels with COVID-19, where individual liberties and sensible precaution have been set up as antagonists. I worry about what it says that two characters in my creative control are willing to die to test a theory. But then I remember YPT Artistic Director Allen MacInnis's voice during one rehearsal, both our eyes a little watery after a monologue by the incredible Kate Martin as Pria. He turned to me and said, "You've written a play about love."

And that meaning hasn't changed. Remembering this permits me to think of Pria and Theo's goal as galaxies apart from the self-appointed defiant: science deniers, hate groups, or those that would take to the streets to protest nurses and doctors who have endured this impossible time that was never as communal as we needed it to be. Pria and Theo's shared rebellion has a different motivation: "it's the love, dingdong," if I may recall a line they share.

Pria and Theo meet in a seedy motel and wade into their unknown, carrying the weight of explorers on a new planet. As I write this in the fall of 2021, we too take small steps on our strange planet as we attempt social, physical, and emotional recovery after a period of intense disconnection from one another and ourselves. In 2019 I wrote, "Stepping out into their new world is less about a fear of dying than it is about a fear of not living." Do I still believe that?

I want each second for Pria and Theo to be as big as possible; as part of that bigness, I knew that opera would be a part of the play, an integral element for characters who want to lengthen time and experience the things they fear they'll miss out on. Opera is exceptionally good at magnifying time and emotion this way. Composer Gareth Williams, who I've worked with for a very fast decade now, consistently wows me with music that holds space for several emotions, but especially love. Love in all its cheesy, logical, passionate, finite, and, yes, operatic forms.

Thank you to Young People's Theatre and now Playwrights Canada Press for seeing the value in a play with opera, where at any moment the love two characters share might cause them to explode into a million billion pieces.

Kaboom.

David James Brock
November 2021

a million billion pieces was commissioned and first produced by Young People's Theatre, Toronto, on November 25, 2019, with the following cast and creative team:

Theo: Aldrin Bundoc
Eagle19: Simon Gagnon
Pria: Kate Martin
PriaSoprano: Jonelle Sills

Director: Philip Akin
Composer: Gareth Williams
Stage Manager: Kate Porter
Set and Costume Design: Rachel Forbes
Lightning Design: Kaitlin Hickey
Production Design: Daniel Oulton
Dramaturg: Stephen Colella
Assistant Director: Samson Bonkeabantu Brown

a million billion pieces is an extension of *Breath Cycle*, an opera project for singers with cystic fibrosis created by Gareth Williams and David James Brock (www.breathcycle.co.uk). Thank you to Scottish Opera for the support at the project's genesis.

This draft is written with the generous support of the Canada Council for the Arts.

notes

Indented text under a character name indicates a sung line associated with the included score. The following would indicate singing:

PRIASOPRANO
Kaboom

English translations from *La bohème* (scene 6) are indicated by quotation marks. All other libretto/lyrics are by Brock and Williams.

All music can be recreated live with a piano and loop station. Alternatively, pre-recorded instrumental tracks would suffice.

Sans-serif text is used to suggest typing/texting/the technology of the day, though it is indeed vocalized. Projections and images, either full or partial, make the online conversations easier to follow. Think Reddit, 4chan . . . giving way to video.

Overlapping dialogue on subsequent lines should begin at double slashes (//).

The action is continuous with sounds and scenes resonating into each other, particularly where words are sung—there should be constant echoes between the scenes (e.g., PriaSoprano's voice resonating in the motel scenes or the Comments Chorus's pervasive supporting, liking, hating).

characters

PRIA: Sixteen. She is layer upon layer. Maybe you find her.
THEO: Sixteen. He'd break if you really touch him.
PRIASOPRANO: A powerful soprano. All her lines are music.
EAGLEI9: A powerful eagle. The canary in a coal mine.
COMMENTS CHORUS: A comments section. Multiple distinct
voices.

setting

A motel somewhere in the universe.
Online.

set

A basic motel room. Some suggestion of a door.
A distinct playing area for online conversations, which will
gradually encroach on the motel.

prologue

Black. We hear PRIASOPRANO's *vocal exercises building from somewhere far off and gradually getting closer.*

SONG 1: VOCAL EXERCISE A

A sudden light reveals an excited EAGLE19, *who interrupts the vocal exercise. He is an eagle in a* NASA-*style astronaut suit. Through the following he is punching holes in a long strip of paper, almost at random.*

EAGLE19
Anyone out there tonight?

Beat.

My family treats me like a canary.

They think I'm . . . sensitive.

EAGLE19 calls up a photo of his uncle Carlos.

I got an uncle, Uncle Carlos, and I hardly know Uncle Carlos, and if you're anything like me, maybe you have an uncle you don't know all that well and who doesn't know you all that well, and if you're reading this, Uncle Carlos, I don't care because—

Whatever. You ain't reading this.

EAGLE19 removes the photo of Uncle Carlos.

This one time, my fam is over at my house—family meal. Chicken. Me, my parents, Uncle Carlos. A dozen cousins. A dozen chickens. Everyone's gotta eat.

The whole place smells like family and chickens and it's hot as a star birth because the oven's been roasting chickens all day. Jam a family in a small space and things'll get star-birth hot. And then . . .

THEO coughs through the following.

I cough and the entire family stops to watch me cough. You all know how that goes, heh?

See, everyone knows I'm sick. Born sick. Knows about the coughing fits. I'm sensitive. A disease of the month. Somethin' you run a 10K to find a cure for.

The fit lasts a minute—sometimes coughing fits last a minute—and that's a long time to have a room stop and pay attention to you when your life goal is to . . . blend.

The coughing stops.

After my fit, it's mad silent.

Fam is surprised I haven't fallen apart.

Cue Uncle Carlos, who cuts the silence, yells to my mother, whose name is Rosa, "Crack a window, Rosa. Your boy's a canary in a coal mine, and soon we'll all be hacking up a lung."

Canary in a coal mine. It's a thing I've never heard. So later that night, house empty, Uncle Carlos has bounced, I look it up.

> EAGLEI9 *types in "Canary in a Coal Mine" and gets millions and billions of hits.*

Before technology, coal miners would bring a canary down into the mine with them.

Coal mining seems like the worst and most dangerous job in the history of the world.

There was something called black lung that the miners could get.

Go check out black lung later. Here's a link.

> EAGLEI9 *gives a hyperlink to "Black Lung."*

If you can't tell by the name "black lung" . . . black lung is a terrible thing to get as a result of your job.

There are two types of diseases, I guess. Ones you're born with (me), and ones you get (coal miners).

Beat.

'Cause the canaries are small, right, sensitive to . . . um . . . sensitive to tiny whatever—particles—so coal miners kept the canaries around to check the air. And if the canary got sick, dead meat usually, the miner knew the air was poison.

So the miner would go get a mask or whatever before the poison could affect him.

So a canary in a coal mine is a warning. A canary in the coal mine lets us know if an uncertain thing is a safe thing, and all it takes is the death of a little ol' canary.

It was like—remember my entry on Laika the Russian space dog a couple of weeks ago? The dog they sent up into space before they sent humans? That was a canary in a coal mine, except in that case, it was a dog . . . in space . . . here, check that one out later. One of my better posts.

He posts a photo of Laika in a spacesuit.

I think the miner just dropped the dead canary on the coal mine floor when he was done with it or whatever.

Beat.

Human history is full of animals going to dangerous places before humans go there. They call these . . . animal sentinels. I'll tell you more about animal sentinels in future posts. Maybe. But check it out if you wanna check it out . . .

EAGLE19 puts up a link on "Animal Sentinels."

Anyone out there tonight?

He gets a like.

Hit me up in the comments.

Beat.

I gotta be somewhere tonight. Somewhere dangerous. Somewhere I can't send a canary. Or Eagle19.

I gotta go as sensitive ol' me.

Until next time, all. If there is a next time. Wish me luck, all. Eagle19 out!

A chorus of voices is heard from off.

COMMENTS CHORUS
Good luck, homey!

You're insane. Total idiot! Praying 4 u!

Rooting for you, bro! Game changer!

Let us know if you explode and die, Eagle19!

EAGLE19 stuffs the strip of paper into a backpack and exits into black the exact moment PRIASOPRANO appears and begins to sing.

PRIASOPRANO
Eagle19? Eagle19? Are you coming?

PRIASOPRANO continues her vocal exercises, alternating with PRIA's countdown.

SONG 2: VOCAL EXERCISE B

PRIA
Five . . . four . . . three . . . two . . . one . . . Kaboom.

PRIASOPRANO
Kaboom!

PRIASOPRANO's song echoes into the cross-fade with the next scene, even as she disappears—something that will happen throughout the play.

one

A motel room, initially only lit by a cellphone. PRIA's face appears over the phone. She texts. The motel room gradually comes into light.

PRIA wipes down the room meticulously with anti-bacterial liquid, but then begins to cough. The coughs cut PRIASOPRANO's song. PRIA wipes the spots she has coughed on.

A knock on the door. PRIA opens it, revealing THEO in a haz-mat suit with a full mask.

PRIA
Theo?

THEO
Uh huh.

PRIA
Overdoing it, ya think?

THEO
You're Pria?

PRIA
You know what I look like, weirdo.

THEO
Pria. Hello.

PRIA
What's with the come-in-peace getup?

THEO
The what?

Beat.

PRIA
So you're here.

THEO
I'm here.

Beat.

PRIA
You've always just been a head on some shoulders. Before that, some lonely words on a screen. Before that, a dream I had.

THEO
Eh?

PRIA spins around.

PRIA
What'cha think?

Beat.

That was stupid.

THEO
What was?

PRIA
Twirling. I'm not like that. I was pretending to be funny.

Beat.

THEO
Do I come in now?

They both look at the motel bed.

PRIA
Take off the gear. You'll have to // eventually.

THEO
I know.

PRIA
Where'd you get that? This . . . suit?

THEO
Haz-mat suit. Hazardous materials.

PRIA
I'm hazardous, eh, bubba?

THEO
We both are.

PRIA
Sexy . . .

THEO
Huh?

PRIA
Get it off and get on in.

THEO *doesn't move.*

THEO
We're still cool for this?

PRIA
You've been cautious your whole life, right? Avoiding people like ourselves because of a theory . . . our whole lives . . . leading up to this moment have been mired in precautions.

THEO
Informed by precautions.

PRIA
Mired.

THEO
Sure, mired. Mired.

PRIA
And where's that got us?

THEO
Here.

PRIA
Right.

THEO
Livin'.

PRIA
Whoopdee for livin'.

THEO
Still breathin'.

PRIA
Livin' the dream. Breathin'.

THEO
In one piece.

    PRIA starts to disrobe a bit.

PRIA
Take that off and get in. Feel like I'm about to lose my virginity to a robot.

THEO
Just . . . slow down.

PRIA
What, you're not horny anymore?

    THEO enters but still does not take off the suit.

The suit.

    THEO doesn't take off the suit.

You don't think in your entire . . . you've never accidentally
been in an elevator or a grocery store or something with someone like us . . .

THEO
Probs. I don't know.

PRIA
And did you explode then? In the elevator? In the dairy aisle?
Just by being close?

THEO
Obviously not.

PRIA
So you're not gonna explode just by being in the room. Our
superbugs aren't laser beams, right?

THEO
No, but—

PRIA
And if we're gonna cause each other to explode into a million billion pieces, we can at least have some fun on our last night on the planet, heh?

THEO
This is some real shit.

PRIA
What did you expect?

THEO
I got no imagination.

PRIA
This was about not being fragile dolls on a glass shelf, right?

THEO
Right.

PRIA
This was the idea . . . this moment. Rebels. Together. Right?

THEO
Together.

PRIA
So let's get at it, stud.

A snap transition to:

two

EAGLE19 appears.

EAGLE19
Anyone out there in the great big . . . universe? I'm having a bad day. Lonely day. I feel like the first dog in space. Anyone know that story?

Pause. He begins to type "First Dog in Space," but PRIASOPRANO *appears in a separate area. She has* PM'd *him.*

"Song 3: Vocal Exercise C" floats within the scene, PRIA *providing a backing for* PRIASOPRANO's *lines where indicated.*

SONG 3: VOCAL EXERCISE C

PRIASOPRANO
Hey, Eagle19. Cool pic. You're a sickie too, heh?

EAGLE19
Yeah.

PRIASOPRANO
I read your posts in here sometimes.

EAGLE19
Least someone does.

We hear PRIA's *vocal exercise.*

PRIASOPRANO
Loved the one about Pluto not being a planet anymore
. . . like it's some outcast.

EAGLE19
Nice to meet.

PRIASOPRANO
You know a lot.

EAGLE19
I dunno, I just look stuff up mostly.

We hear PRIA's *vocal exercise.*

PRIASOPRANO
What's your name mean?

EAGLE19
I dig eagles. What about you?

PRIASOPRANO
I am PriaSoprano . . . the greatest singer in the universe!

EAGLE19
The universe is pretty big.

PRIASOPRANO
Duh. I'm not stupid.

EAGLE19
Sorry. Didn't mean it like that. I just like that sort of stuff.

PRIASOPRANO
What sort of stuff?

EAGLE19
Universe stuff.

>   *We hear* PRIA's *vocal exercise.*

PRIASOPRANO
Haha. "Universe stuff." So like . . . you like EVERYTHING?

EAGLE19
Yeah, I know.

PRIASOPRANO
(building to a vocal flourish on "big") The universe is pretty big 🌑

>   PRIA *and* PRIASOPRANO *share a vocal exercise.*

>   *A snap transition back to the motel.*

three

PRIA goes into her bag and pulls out a large plastic drop cloth. She covers the bed with it.

PRIA
There, just in case. Save the maid some trouble. Respect.

THEO
People call me tragic. I ain't.

PRIA
Okay.

THEO
But people think—

PRIA
People are the worst. So what?

THEO
I just want you to know . . . I plan on walking out of here in one piece.

PRIA
You think?

THEO
I hope.

PRIA
Okay. Whatever, we're not Romeo and Juliet, I get it.

THEO
They die in the end.

PRIA
Lucky them.

THEO
You're really okay with the idea that this might be the last thing we ever do before we blow up into a million billion pieces? On the wall and the bed and the plastic sheet—

PRIA
And so what if we did? Explode. Die. So what? What's the big deal?

THEO
I think I'm gonna bounce.

PRIA
Chickenshit. No wonder all your stories are about how lonely you are.

THEO
They're not really stories—

PRIA
You're scared to *not* be lonely. So here I am!

THEO
Later, Pria.

But he doesn't move. She sees this.

PRIA
You need to chill. I didn't mean it like—like no one remembers that Romeo and Juliet died. They remember their love.

THEO
Their love?

PRIA
Yeah, the love part is the reason we take it in school, right? To learn how to love, or what love is . . .

THEO
Love, though?

PRIA
Though maybe they just teach it as a big old sex warning. Like, Romeo and Juliet died. And people been telling us that we can't be together or we'll explode into a million billion pieces. Like— it's all nonsense. Parents and teachers gotta have something better to do, right? I mean it's not just sickies. It's everyone our age. Pregnancy. Sex. AIDS. Sex. Sex. And okay, us . . . Kaboom— sex. Scary scary sex!

THEO
Scary.

PRIA
And I don't care what you say, Theo—in Romeo and Juliet, love meant sex. No waiting around. They boned for sure. And then they died, and good for them for getting sex out of the way before they bit it.

Pause.

THEO
You keep saying love.

PRIA
Yeah, their love, dingdong.

THEO
Is that what this is about, 'cause I didn't think—uh—we—

PRIA
We don't have to be in love for this to be meaningful.

THEO
Okay.

PRIA
And anyways, Romeo and Juliet were only thirteen or fourteen. We're ancient compared to them.

Snap.

four

EAGLE19 appears.

PRIASOPRANO appears. We hear "Song 4: Vocal Exercise D" with both PRIA and PRIASOPRANO contributing. As in Scene Two, we hear PRIA float within the scene, providing a backing for PRIASOPRANO's lines where indicated. However, the music starts to gain in volume/urgency.

SONG 4: VOCAL EXERCISE D

EAGLE19
You came back.

PRIASOPRANO
Of course I did.

EAGLE19
Some chicks get scared.

We hear PRIA's vocal exercise.

PRIASOPRANO
Maybe 'cause you call them chicks, dude.

EAGLE19
I'm sorry. I'm bad at this.

PRIASOPRANO
Not a big Casanova, eh?

EAGLE19
Who's that?

       PRIASOPRANO links him "Casanova."

PRIASOPRANO
Oh . . . I've stumped the great mind of Eagle19!

    We hear PRIA's vocal exercise.

Casanova was just some guy who was with lots of chicks a few hundred years ago.

EAGLE19
Seems sort of gross.

PRIASOPRANO
You think so?

EAGLE19
What do I know?

PRIASOPRANO
You're not like other boys.

EAGLE19

Yeah . . . duh. Been told that like since birth.

THEO coughs.

PRIASOPRANO

Chill, dude. This is a compliment.

EAGLE19

Sorry. I told you, I'm bad at this. I'm no . . . Casa Loma.

PRIASOPRANO

Nova.

EAGLE19

Like supernova.

We hear PRIA's vocal exercise.

PRIASOPRANO

What's a supernova?

EAGLE19 links her "Supernova."

EAGLE19

Like when a star dies . . . it explodes . . . it gets really bright
. . . and . . .

PRIASOPRANO

Kaboom?

EAGLE19
Then it's gone.

    Beat.

PRIASOPRANO
Kaboom.

    Beat.

EAGLE19
My heart was racing all day at school . . . thinking about us chatting tonight.

PRIASOPRANO
And now?

EAGLE19
Heart feels like it's gonna kaboom out of my body . . .

PRIASOPRANO
Kaboom!

EAGLE19
I've never felt this all over the place.

PRIASOPRANO
Danger!

EAGLE19
Circling danger.

PRIASOPRANO
Ya never been close to dying.

EAGLE19
Like not . . . *dangerously* close.

PRIASOPRANO
What kind of sickie are you? 🌑

EAGLE19
You've been close?

PRIASOPRANO
Just a supernova waiting to happen.

Pause. From the motel . . .

THEO
My name is Theo . . . IRL.

PRIA
I'm Pria. IRL. Obvs.

Pause. Will they go on?

EAGLE19
So, Pria . . . do anything dangerous today?

We hear the power of PRIASOPRANO'S *vocal exercise.*

Snap.

five

The motel. As before.

THEO
You think it's happened?

PRIA
What?

THEO
Think we've given each other superbugs?

PRIA
Well, if it happens, I want the end to come fast. That it's not this . . . slow . . . we've lived with all our lives. I hope it's quick . . . big. KABOOM!

THEO
Come on . . .

Beat.

PRIA
Maybe you should take off the spacesuit . . . let your superbugs go for a spin, big boy.

THEO
Pria?

PRIA
Don't do that.

THEO
Do what?

PRIA
Say my name as a question and just my name and nothing else while you wait for me to say "what" so that you can just say what you wanna say. Just say what you wanna say and don't feel like you have to tee me up about it with my name in the form of a question.

THEO
Sorry.

PRIA
We need to be more efficient about this. I'm sick, Theo.

THEO
Uh, duh—

PRIA
No. I mean . . . whether I explode tonight or not . . . the clock is ticking on this bod.

    Beat.

So take your space pants off.

THEO
This isn't a real haz-mat suit. It's just like . . . a Halloween costume.

THEO takes of the mask, revealing his face for the first time. The rest of the suit stays on.

PRIA
Nice to meet you, Theo.

They shake hands. Their first touch, but through a glove.

Theo?

THEO
What?

PRIA
Annoying, isn't it?

THEO pulls his hand back.

THEO
I got you something.

PRIA
Like a present?

THEO
Yeah.

THEO goes into his backpack and pulls out the strip of paper he had been making holes in as EAGLEI9. He hands her the paper.

PRIA
Uh . . . cool? What is it?

THEO
I know you like music. It's music. Here . . .

THEO goes back into his bag and pulls out a hand-cranked music box. He puts the paper in. The paper strip must be hand-punched prior to this scene as a c major arpeggio, similar to the loops and exercises.

Turn the crank.

PRIA does and pretty music escapes. The sound grows from the instrument and fills the space with a slowed-down recording of the music box. It washes over them for a moment, and they continue as the music plays.

PRIA
It's beautiful. Thank you.

THEO
I thought you'd like it.

Beat.

PRIA

Haven't exploded yet. What do the dumb doctors know, huh?

THEO

Is that true? The clock ticking thing you said—like, you're sick
. . . like, for real . . . close—

PRIA

Don't ya ever think about . . . what a relief it would be . . .

The music stops. They are face to face.

That if I just kiss you . . . if my spit and your spit touch
. . . maybe and finally . . .

Kaboom.

Snap.

six

EAGLE19 appears.

EAGLE19
How was your day today, PriaSoprano?

Silence.

How was your day today, PriaSoprano?

Silence.

PRIASOPRANO appears. She's been listening to sad opera all day. La bohème.

PRIASOPRANO
Do you think we're special?

EAGLE19
What do you mean?

PRIASOPRANO
Do you think sickies are special?

EAGLE19
I dunno.

PRIASOPRANO
Do you know *La bohème*? It's an opera.

EAGLE19
No. I'll listen to it tonight. For sure. Link me?

She links him "La bohème." It continues to play softly throughout the following.

PRIASOPRANO
There's this character Mimì. Everyone loves her. But she's dying right from the very beginning of the opera. It makes people love her more. Do you think that's real?

Beat.

Like, okay . . . how about this. Do you know anything about genetics?

EAGLE19
Obvs.

PRIASOPRANO
Like how if a kid gets blue eyes and his parents don't have blue eyes . . .

EAGLE19
Yeah, I know. Recessive genes. His parents carry the gene but don't show it . . . like our okay parents who didn't explode, but did it and made us . . .

PRIASOPRANO
Okay, know-it-all . . .

EAGLE19
Sorry . . .

PRIASOPRANO
The one thing I don't like about you is how much you apologize.

SONG 5: PUNNETT SQUARE MUSIC INTO LA BOHÈME EXCERPT (ARRANGED BY WILLIAMS)

A Punnett square projection starts to take shape through the following, PRIASOPRANO creates them, piece by piece, with each block filling in at her command (and eventually EAGLE19's) until the letters become emojis:

So our parents weren't like us. They were okay.

	C	c
C		
c		

The odds of them meeting was like one in a million.

	C	c
C	CC	Cc
c	Cc	**cc**

Then the odds of them having us were one in four.

	C	c
C	OK	OK
c	OK	**cc**

Then the odds of us meeting was another . . . like . . . one in a billion.

	C	c
C		
c		"us"

Okay, so maybe that only makes us . . . rare.

EAGLE19

We're unique. Lucky us. Like the odds of winning the lottery.

😵 + 😦 = 😵😵

PRIASOPRANO

This is a pretty crappy prize.

EAGLE19

But like . . . imagine two sickies had a baby? Like if sickies could even touch . . .

Another Punnett square projection starts to take shape through the following . . .

I mean, think about it . . .

	c	c
c		
c		

We'd know exactly what would happen.

	c	c
c	cc	cc
c	cc	cc

When's the last time you were certain about anything?

	C	C
C		
C		

Aren't you tired of the mystery? Of nothing being in our control?

PRIASOPRANO
You got us going from virgins to parents crazy quick.

EAGLE19
Hey, who said I was a virgin?!

PRIASOPRANO
It's okay, Eagle19. I am too!

PRIASOPRANO sings.

PRIASOPRANO
   "They speak to me of
   love."

                              EAGLE19
                              What's that?

PRIASOPRANO
It's *La bohème* . . . listen.

> "Of fancies and
> visions bright they tell
> me / such as poets
> and only poets know.
> Do you hear me?"

It's the moment in the opera
where Mimì and Rodolpho
meet for the first time
and they instantly fall in
love . . .

> "Spring's first sweet
> fragrant kiss is mine.
> / It's mine."

Can I meet you?

EAGLE19
I've never done this.

PRIASOPRANO
Will you meet me?

EAGLE19
I've never done this!

Snap.

seven

They are still close.

THEO
I've never . . . done this.

PRIA
I know.

THEO
Like . . .

PRIA
It's called sex, Theo.

THEO giggles, and if there was a spell, it's broken.

And if you can't say it, you're not supposed to have it.

THEO
I can say it.

Pause. Then, weirdly . . .

Sex.

PRIA
You got a condom?

> THEO *finally takes off the haz-mat suit and digs into his pockets.*

THEO
Uh huh. My dad gave me three.

PRIA
Three. You cowboy.

THEO
Said that if a superbug was gonna get me, it was gonna be the ones I was born with, not the ones I got on my pecker.

PRIA
Hey! I'm not like that.

THEO
I know. I know.

PRIA
He said pecker?

THEO
Uh huh.

PRIA
Weird. Pecker. And weird. Them letting you meet me when they knew that if we . . . did *this* . . . we might both shatter into a . . .

THEO
What'd your mom say?

PRIA
(*evading*) We should kiss now.

THEO
You're psyched to explode, heh?

PRIA
So you *really* believe it, then? That eventually, by some magic, you and I will cause each other to explode?

THEO
Maybe.

PRIA
Me too.

THEO
Yeah.

PRIA
But still, you came here.

THEO
So did you.

PRIA
But now . . .

THEO
No one else has ever tried this. We're the first.

PRIA
So then? Rebels!

THEO
Sorry. I'm just—

PRIA
(*playful turn*) Don't be sorry, I'm hot A F—you wanted some of dis!

    Beat.

You were gonna risk your life for me.

    Beat.

Until you got here.

    Beat.

Am I too pale?

THEO
Are you pale?

PRIA
Too sick looking?

THEO
We're both sick *looking.*

PRIA
But I'm closer to the end—

THEO
Don't say that.

PRIA
And you're different than I thought too, bud. Like, I didn't even know your height . . .

THEO
Sorry. Am I disappointing?

PRIA
No.

THEO
Okay, I'm not sorry then.

> *Beat.*

Say we don't explode—

PRIA
Meh.

THEO
If we don't explode, I believe things can get better.

PRIA

Everyone believes their life will get better. Almost never happens.
You get a best day, then everything after that is a giant letdown.

THEO

What was your best day?

PRIA

This was supposed to be. Sex. Explode. Die.

THEO

You don't think they can cure us?

PRIA

It.

THEO

It. Whatever.

PRIA

There's no cure // for it.

THEO

I don't think that. All sorts of things that used to kill people
don't. Chicken pox.

PRIA

And you'd just as easily // find . . .

THEO

The bubonic plague—

PRIA

. . . a cure for being too tall.

Beat.

THEO

A hacksaw.

PRIA

Say what?

THEO

A hacksaw would cure height. Like, say someone was too tall.
You could hacksaw yourself down . . . maybe at the ankles. The
shins. The knees. All problems got a solution. Eventually.

PRIA

You're stupid.

THEO

So are you.

PRIA

So, what—if we don't explode, you're asking me on a
second date?

THEO

Yes.

PRIA

Kiss my mouth.

THEO
Pria?

PRIA
Theo?

THEO
Don't do that.

PRIA
I'm tired.

THEO
I know. Me too.

PRIA
Kill me?

THEO
What?

PRIA
Please kill me before I die.

She goes to kiss him.

He steps back.

Snap.

eight

PRIASOPRANO and EAGLE19. Through the following we hear PRIA struggling through her vocal warm-ups.

SONG 6: PRIA'S HOSPITAL SONG

PRIASOPRANO

I like you. You make me laugh. You make me look forward.
You make me afraid.
I fear the day we meet face to face.
I fear the day we're in the same place.
I fear the day you wish we never met.
I have never known anyone for a very long time,
and it breaks my heart in two.
I believe this. One day we'll meet.
And then we'll kiss, and explode into pieces.
A million billion pieces.
I have never known anyone for a very long time.

But I'll sign off now.
I'll go offline. Leave this chat behind.
And live in the real world.

EAGLE19

Wait, where are you going?

PRIASOPRANO

I believe this.
If I get through the next few days,
You will count the ways I'm coming for you.
We're just getting started.
We're just getting started.
We're just getting started.
We're just getting started.

PRIA shows herself to EAGLE19.

PRIA

I'm going into the hospital for a while. Thanks for the dope
year, Theo.

PRIA coughs into black. And disappears.

EAGLE19

PriaSoprano? You still there? Hello?

Beat.

We were just getting started.

A slow transition this time.

nine

As before. THEO *doesn't move in.*

PRIA
Okay, if you're not gonna do this—I'll find someone else.

THEO
What do you mean *someone else*?

PRIA
Some other sickie.

THEO
You talk to sickies other than me?

PRIA
Maybe.

THEO
I can't leave you like this.

PRIA
Like what?

THEO
All like . . . suicidal.

PRIA
It's not suicide if it's gonna happen anyway. It's power.

THEO
Your mom would be mad pissed.

PRIA
Two weeks ago my mom was saying goodbye forever to me in a hospital.

THEO
Where did you tell her you were going tonight?

PRIA
Out.

THEO
That's so cold.

PRIA
Well, not all our parents are as perfect as yours, dude.

THEO
She's gotta be worried about you . . .

PRIA
Knock it off.

THEO
It's selfish.

PRIA
Save the crap.

THEO
People worry about us because they love us.

PRIA
If only we were all as strong as you . . .

    THEO *horks into his hand. It's bloody.*

THEO
That look strong to you?

    Beat.

PRIA
You worried about me, Romeo?

THEO
Yeah.

    PRIA *tenderly wipes the blood from his hand with a tissue,*
    careful to still not make skin-to-skin contact.

PRIA
Every time I've ever coughed in my entire life, every sniffle,
comes with a gasp from my mom. I cough. She gasps. I cough
three times. You can practically hear it. Gasp-gasp-gasp . . . She

never got used to this broken thing she got saddled with. My older sister is okay. She's the good one. I'm the porcelain doll on the glass shelf. And we said, that tonight, we were gonna come here and be rebels—to be our own astronauts.

THEO
Pilot our own ships.

PRIA
And now you're looking at me like she looks at me, you asshole.

THEO
My ma cried when I told her I was coming here. She believes . . . kaboom. My dad shook my hand. He believes . . . I might. They asked if they could pick me up after. I told them I didn't know how long we'd be. I'd take a taxi or a bus or hitch a ride on the back of an eagle or a rocket ship . . .

I get it, Pria.

I feel—I know that their lives will be easier when I'm gone. Whether it's a year from now or at some point tonight . . .

PRIA
Kaboom.

THEO
Kaboom.

PRIA
Some okay parents get kids who might explode, and some okay parents get kids who, like, sleep with everyone on the basketball team.

THEO
Yeah.

Wait. What?

PRIA
Nothing. Rumour at my high school.

Silence. THEO *pulls out two cigarettes.*

THEO
Oh, hey—my dad also gave me these.

PRIA
Maybe they really do want you dead.

THEO
It's just a couple of smokes. A couple of smokes never killed anyone, even a couple of sickies like us. I see sickies smoking outside the hospital all the time. Ever smoked?

PRIA
I've been to parties, you know. I'm not a kid.

THEO
So you've drank, too?

PRIA
I like the taste of gin in my mouth and how it feels in my throat and stomach and when my fingers tingle. When they . . . fingle.

THEO
Drugs?

PRIA
Weed. Yeah.

THEO
You've done it all then.

PRIA
Hardly call that "it all" . . .

THEO
More than me.

PRIA
What, you don't have a list of things to do before the end?

THEO
No. Why, do you?

PRIA
Sure.

THEO
Like bungee jumping?

PRIA
Go see the Maria Callas sculpture.

THEO
That's . . . an opera thing . . .

PRIA
Singer.

THEO
An opera singer?

PRIA
She's *the* opera singer. And there's this sculpture of her in Athens. Greece. I wanted to travel to see it.

THEO
Greece. Warm there.

PRIA
Really warm.

THEO
They got Greeks there.

PRIA
Sure. But I basically did none of the things.

An awkward pause. THEO *is examining her inquisitively.*

What is *this* you're doing?

THEO
Huh?

PRIA
It's not hot.

THEO
I don't follow . . .

PRIA
You're stalling. Engaged. Trying to keep me talking. Did you see this on some show where a cop tries to keep a nutcase from jumping off a bridge or something?

THEO
'Scuse me if I can't ask questions of the girl I'm supposed to make love to—

PRIA
Blech. Make love.

THEO
Who is asking me to kill her by making love to her—

PRIA
Don't say make love.

THEO
And perhaps myself in the process of *making love* . . .

PRIA
Dude.

THEO
Explode into . . .

Pause.

Why me?

PRIA
Because . . . you're my boyfriend.

THEO
(*monumental for him*) I am?

PRIA
Aren't you? We've known each other a year. Told each other stuff. You do that with any other bitches?

THEO
Nah.

Beat.

PRIA
Romantic, eh, Romeo?

THEO
You want a cigarette or what?

PRIA
It's a no-smoking room.

THEO
Never heard of a rebel who let a little no-smoking sticker tell her what to do.

PRIA
Give me one then, jerk.

THEO gives her a cigarette. They light them. A fire burns.

Both begin coughing fits after an inhale. They cough on the room, on each other. They put the cigs out quickly.

THEO
Well, the place is crawling with superbugs now.

PRIA
Your saliva is definitely in my mouth.

Pause. They wait. No explosion.

THEO
Still in one piece.

THEO reaches out and takes PRIA's hand. Skin-on-skin contact. Big moment.

Snap.

ten

EAGLE19.

EAGLE19
Anyone out there tonight?

 Beat.

Anyone out there in the big ol' universe?

COMMENTS CHORUS
She's probably dead, dude.

EAGLE19
I was reading about the first dog sent into space. Her name was Laika. Here's a picture.

 EAGLE19 shares the Laika picture.

This was in the 1950s. Russians. They found Laika on the streets of Moscow.

Nineteen-fifties Moscow looked like a rough place to be for people and dogs. Take a look at some of these.

EAGLE19 shows a bunch of old Moscow photos.

The Russians were in a race with the US to send a person to space, but they couldn't send a person at that point, too dangerous, so they sent Laika on November 3, 1957 . . . up on a ship called *Sputnik 2*.

The day before they sent Laika into orbit, one of the *Sputnik 2* scientists took her home so that Laika could play with his kids. He said, "I wanted to do something nice for her, she had so little time left to live," but he said it in Russian.

When I was born, doctors said I wouldn't live past my teens.

COMMENTS CHORUS
Join the club, man.

EAGLE19
That my life expectancy was nineteen. So . . . Eagle19. Get it? No one thinks I'll survive the journey.

But Laika didn't survive the journey.

She died within a few hours.

But the Russians learned a lot by sending up Laika.

Not how to bring her back alive or anything, but they learned something that would help keep humans safe, because in 1961 the Russians put the first man up there. A man named Yuri Gagarin.

I bet some of ya thought it was an American or something.

But Yuri Gagarin was in space for just under two hours and orbited Earth once.

He came home, unharmed, and got his own Russian holiday and Russian statues and buildings with his name on them.

Fifty years later, they built a statue of Laika in Moscow. So that's pretty good.

> *He shows a picture of the Laika statue.*

Picture Laika all alone on that spaceship. Maybe knowing she was taking her last breath. Thinking about how yesterday she was playing with those kids. It all makes me pretty sad.

The saddest stories always involve someone being alone, don't you think? Anyone ever feel like that?

PriaSoprano . . . I need to know you're out there.

> *Beat. Nothing.*

COMMENTS CHORUS
She'll pull through, man.

If she's dead, she's lucky, dude!

Hey Eagle19, check your DM!

EAGLEI9 opens a photo. It's a photo of a dog skeleton labelled "Laika Now."

EAGLEI9 quickly closes it. Shuts off his computer.

Some LOLs from the COMMENTS CHORUS.

Snap.

eleven

As before. Touching hands.

THEO
You said there were other sickies you coulda done this with.
Really?

PRIA
No. Not really.

THEO
So you couldn't have done this with anyone else?

PRIA
What, kill myself?

THEO
No. Sex in motel rooms.

PRIA
That I could obviously do.

THEO
Who?

PRIA
No one you know.

THEO
Obvs, but tell me about one of them.

PRIA
A math boy was kissing my neck at a party once.

THEO
Okay.

PRIA
He started to feel me up.

THEO
Okay.

PRIA
Are you enjoying this?

THEO
If I said yes, would you think I was a pervert?

PRIA
Yes.

THEO
I like it.

PRIA
Pervert.

THEO
Keep going.

PRIA
He freaked out 'cause I tasted like lemons and batteries.

THEO
That's funny.

PRIA
But you're not laughing.

THEO
I mean, I get it. Like . . . I'm sour too. Like people don't know anything about how people like us are sour, so it'd be weird to taste our sour.

    THEO *licks his own sour arm.*

Yep. Lemons.

PRIA
You sour . . . ?

    Nodding down.

THEO
Pervert.

PRIA
Math dude didn't know how I would possibly not break if he got on top of me.

THEO
I know you won't break.

PRIA
Then why are you so afraid to get on with this? Are you *obsessed* with living?

THEO
I'm not obsessed, I just don't want to die.

PRIA
Dude, why did you // even come here?

THEO
I don't wanna die a virgin!

PRIA
Well, you're doing a terrible job at fulfilling your life goals—!

THEO
Do you think I'm good-looking?

PRIA
I'm here, aren't I?

THEO
Rank me. One to ten.

PRIA
That's stupid.

THEO
So under five?

PRIA
No, listen. You're beautiful. I like that I see in you what people see in me. Like . . . that fragility.

THEO
Great.

PRIA
Like, you could crush a butterfly but still think it's beautiful, right?

THEO
What about me is beautiful?

PRIA
Don't be needy.

THEO
Get me in the mood. I need to know that you actually like me if I'm gonna do this.

PRIA
Your face.

THEO
What about it?

PRIA
It's got a nice shape.

THEO
Which shape?

PRIA
I like how your neck is, like, this long rectangle. And your head is oval. And they are two completely separate shapes. The oval just sits on the rectangle, like an egg on top of a like . . . paper-towel roll.

THEO
So I'm skinny.

PRIA
And you have a pointy chin.

THEO
I always wanted muscles.

PRIA
You're fragile and beautiful, now shut the hell up.

Beat.

The way your shoulders hunch forward a bit. Like mine. I think it's ugly that boys are raised to stand with their shoulders back as though everyone is Superman or on the basketball team.

Beat.

So, what about me, then? Put me in the mood. You think I'm good-looking?

THEO
I think so.

PRIA
You are so bad at this.

THEO
I wouldn't ogle you on the street.

PRIA
You don't think I'm ogle-able?

THEO
You wanna be?

PRIA
Sometimes, but like—respectably. My sister is ogle-able.
Total babe.

> PRIA *shows* THEO *a photo of her sister on her phone.*

THEO
She's okay.

PRIA
You have bad taste.

THEO
If I focus on it, on your prettiness, I see it. But that's not why I
love—why I'm here.

PRIA
Overall, I like the way I look.

THEO
I look forward to the time we have together when I can learn you more.

PRIA
We don't have time.

THEO
I want to know you for a very long time, Pria.

PRIA
(*deflecting the attempt at romance*) I wish I was a little fatter.

THEO
I'm not saying this right. Why is this so hard?

PRIA
Come over here. Let me help you.

THEO begins approaching PRIA, a magnet between them.

I dreamed us. Before I found you. Together. In this exact moment.

THEO
You have?

PRIA
There's a little countdown. There's some music. The ceiling disappears and then a white fire. And it doesn't hurt. In the white fire.

THEO
Really?

PRIA
And it doesn't hurt.

THEO
A supernova . . .

PRIA
And if it does, not for long. And not worse than anything I'm not already feeling—or anything you've already felt—only this time. Kaboom.

THEO
Kaboom.

PRIA
Kaboom.

They are as close as they've ever been.

Kiss me.

THEO
Okay.

THEO kisses her. It's happening!

Snap.

twelve

EAGLE19 alone. THE COMMENTS CHORUS starts slow, then becomes a cacophony—chaotic as star birth—some repeated, before they trail off again.

COMMENTS CHORUS
Face it, dude, she's gone.

What's it been, like two weeks?

Stop crying. None of us are happy.

Maybe she met another dude in here and they tried to meet up and THEY exploded!

I'll chat with ya, Eagle19.

I have a project on Saturn's moons due tomorrow. Can you help me out?

Cutie.

It's not like you were ever gonna meet her for real.

Hottie.

Check your DM, Eagle19.

Don't waste what little time you have worrying. Go for a walk. See a sunset.

God will take care of us.

Check your DM, Eagle19.

I'd say check the obituaries, but you don't even know her last name.

My sister didn't even make it to ten. Grow up.

My brother didn't even make it to eight.

Six! Five! Four!

Two!

My brother was aborted!

Kaboom!

Check your DM, Eagle19.

> *EAGLE19 opens his DM folder. It's the Laika-skeleton photo again, only now someone has written "PriaSoprano Now" under it.*

EAGLE19 & THEO
(rage) If I ever see any of you, I'll fucking kill you!

Comments scatter, and then . . . a lone voice.

COMMENTS CHORUS
If you ever see any of us—we'd explode into a million billion pieces.

The COMMENTS CHORUS laughs.

Snap.

thirteen

They are still kissing as the lights come up. She stops.

THEO
Why are you stopping?

PRIA
Shit. It didn't work. Should've known.

THEO
What, you only kissed me because—

PRIA
Don't be stupid.

> *She kisses him again. She barely moves away from him during the following.*

This is Carla the Soprano in a Starbucks all over again.

THEO
The what?

PRIA
I swear I told you this story.

THEO

We haven't told each other everything. We still got some places to go.

PRIA

It's nothing.

THEO

Okay.

PRIA

That's not true. It's not nothing.

Beat.

THEO

So . . . take me there?

Through the following we hear "Song 7: Pria Takes us to the Opera." Five years earlier. The motel becomes the opera's set.

SONG 7: PRIA TAKES US TO THE OPERA

PRIA

She was this opera singer I saw . . . When I was in junior high, my mom took me to the opera at the Four Seasons. You know it?

THEO

Like . . . I know the building.

PRIA

And it was old-timey but it was in English. And until then I thought all opera had to be Italian or German.

THEO

I always thought my coughs sounded a bit German. You know. Hard. And everyone else coughed politely in like . . . English or French.

PRIA

Sneezes are definitely French.

PRIASOPRANO is in the bed, a young woman dreaming.

And I can't remember what it was called, but I remember this part near the end . . . the orchestra just rocked back and forward, and the woman, she was having this dream. About someone she liked. A lot. Like a lover. His name was . . . Armando or something.

PRIASOPRANO hums "Armando" beautifully.

But then it was interrupted.

The FATHER enters (played by the same actor as EAGLE19).
He vocalizes his lines in bold, stealing them from PRIA.

It was her father. And he wakes her up and says, **"Today is the day you will marry."**

THEO

Married to the guy she loves in the dream? Armando?

PRIA

Of course not. It's opera, dude. She says,

PRIASOPRANO

No. No, no, no, no. I love another.

PRIA

But he says, **"You will do this. You will not shame this family. You will be his wife."** And she shrinks in front of him. Like a tiny pebble. Right there on the bed.

And the way that man was making her feel . . . I knew that feeling exactly. I felt it all the time. Powerless. Absolutely powerless. And I couldn't look away from her.

THEO

So what happened?

PRIASOPRANO

Okay. Okay. I will marry him.
Okay. Okay, I will do as you say.
Okay, okay, I'll marry him.

FATHER relents and is happy.

PRIA

So later that day . . . he proposes "**a toast.**" He has won and she will do as he says. As she always has. And she goes to pour him a drink.

What he doesn't see though . . . is that she puts poison into the wine bottle.

PRIASOPRANO spikes the bottle of wine with poison.

THEO
No way.

PRIA's narration carries the action of the following opera scene.

PRIA
Soooo opera. And she brings him his drink.

And he says, "**To my daughter on her wedding day. To doing your duty. And may you do the next man's bidding better than you did mine.**"

He takes a gulp! But then he pours her a glass in return. She pauses for a second . . . and then . . . drains the glass and smiles.

Her father is happy. He has won . . . for the moment. Until . . .

FATHER falls to his knees, the poison taking its effect.

PRIASOPRANO
(*triumphant*) You think I am small and weak.
You think that I am shy and meek.
I have known the love of dreams.
I have known the roar of lions.
I've known the heat of a thousand suns
that burn! That burn!
That burn while you sleep.
Sleep now, Father. Sleep now.
And may you burn.

PRIA
The father dies.

> *PRIASOPRANO begins to feel the poison. She gets herself back into bed to end as she began, in her beautiful dream (humming "Armando").*

Then she starts to feel the poison. She goes back to the bed. Back to a dream. Back to her lover.

PRIASOPRANO
> (*softly*) Soft and sweetly. You will be
> there waiting, waiting for me.
> Strong and silent. You will be there
> with me. I know the love of dreams,
> and now I dream forever.

PRIA
Her last beautiful breath escaped, and changed the whole world around her.

PRIASOPRANO & PRIA
(*whispered*) Kaboom.

> *PRIASOPRANO dies comfortably in bed.*

THEO
Holy shit.

> *A silence.*

PRIA
I went home that night and cried into my pillow. Decided I would take singing lessons.

THEO
And . . .

PRIA
I'll never sing opera.

Beat.

THEO
So what's the soprano Starbucks thing then?

PRIA
I saw her there. The singer. The daughter . . . Like . . . a week after or something. She was cool. She looked different on stage than she did at Starbucks.

THEO
Was she too short?

PRIASOPRANO and PRIA in the Starbucks. They play out the following flashback, not regarding THEO.

PRIA
I recognize you. You're a beautiful singer.

PRIASOPRANO hugs PRIA.

PRIASOPRANO
Thank you.

The hug holds. Then PRIASOPRANO *exits.*

THEO
Very cool. So then a happy ending?

PRIA
No, because it 100% confirmed that she was nothing like me.
Because I thought that if she could touch me, and we didn't
explode . . .

THEO
She wasn't one of us.

PRIA
I was young. I believed the dumb doctors even more than I do
now. Like, I believed maybe you coming here . . .

THEO
Dumb doctors.

THEO goes to kiss PRIA. *She stops him with—*

PRIA
That was the worst day of my life.

THEO
Oh.

PRIA
I think about that all the time. Because she was special. And if I could touch her . . . it meant someone like me . . . wasn't special.

    PRIASOPRANO's song is miles from the room.

THEO
Sing for me.

PRIA
No.

THEO
I bet you're great.

PRIA
I don't have the power.

THEO
You have mega power.

PRIA
Shut up.

THEO
Sing for me.

PRIA
No. I'm not going to do that.

THEO
Please?

PRIA
No!

THEO
Why not?

PRIA
(*abruptly*) Fly for me, Eagle19.

   Beat.

Life was supposed to be shorter than this. But life just keeps happening. And the longer it goes on . . . I don't know what to do with this time—like when you came in, I was ready to die. And then we start talking . . . and you have me believing that I could know you for a long time. And I hate that . . . because it's not the way things were supposed to be for us.

THEO
You're scared.

PRIA
Of course, you asshole. Death sucks ass.

THEO
We're making progress. A few minutes ago you were ready to explode. Now . . . you're afraid to go . . . that's good. 'Cause now, we get to hang out longer.

   A long pause.

Yeah . . . we're constantly going so much farther than we thought we could.

At this rate, we'll end up in outer space.

Beat.

PRIA
Let's go to Pluto.

THEO
Cool.

PRIA
We're not getting out of this room, are we?

THEO
I don't know.

PRIA
I'm afraid. Super afraid. To leave you now.

Snap.

fourteen

EAGLE19 as before. Alone, bored, sad.

He receives a DM, but hesitates to open it. He does anyway.

It's a video: PRIA from a hospital bed.

PRIA
Hey, Eagle19. It's me. Again. PriaSoprano. But like . . . actually
. . . sorry for the way I look. This is me at my very worst. Sorry.
But hi. Sorry I haven't been in touch. Almost died a few times in
the past couple weeks. Was kinda busy almost dying again.

Think I'm getting outta here soon.

Let's meet. In person. Whatta ya think? Tick tock.

Bye. xo. Pria.

PRIA disappears.

EAGLE19 plays the message again . . .

Snap.

fifteen

The motel.

THEO
So what now?

PRIA
I didn't think this far ahead.

THEO
I convinced myself I was okay with it, you know—coming here. Okay with exploding like everyone said we would. I wasn't really that ready for it.

PRIA
You were brave, Theo.

THEO
I think bravery is just stupidity that didn't get busted. Like, people who jump outta planes, that's stupid. Bungee jumpers, that's stupid. Guy jumps off a bridge tied to a rope. Dumb. Sometimes the rope breaks. And when it breaks, people go, "That guy is stupid." And when it doesn't break, it's the rope doing the work, and they go, "Ohhhh, what a hero." The rope is doing everything all the time!

PRIA musters a smile.

PRIA
Good one.

THEO
When I was little, I used to think God put me into the hospital for being bad.

PRIA
You never said you believed in God. Do I know *anything* about you?

THEO
And I'd act really good. I'd be nice to my ma, help around the house, try to hold in my coughs so I wouldn't bother her, try to pray the sickness from my blood and lungs and stomach.

PRIA
Sounds like you believe in God, dude.

THEO
I believe that after this you get something way better.

PRIA
I'm coming back as a lion.

THEO
And like when praying didn't work, or when I started puking even worse, or having to go to hospitals, no matter what I asked for or did—no, that was my proof. Ain't no God looking at me. Peace out, God.

Things are heavy. Lighten it up. A playful few beats here.

PRIA
This is a hell of a first date, Theo.

THEO
I'm having fun, how about you? Tell me about yourself, Pria.

PRIA
Well, I want to be a doctor someday.

THEO
Me too!

PRIA
What's your specialty?

THEO
Dying kids.

PRIA
You gotta have goals.

THEO
And where do you see yourself in five years?

> *PRIA is instantly back to heavy. THEO takes a few lines to catch up.*

PRIA
Everyone used to tell me I needed goals.

THEO

Right. Your bucket list. Travel to that statue in Greece.

PRIA

Yeah, but I never called it a bucket list. The whole kicking-the-bucket thing felt too jokey. So I called it my Scintilla List.

THEO

Scintilla. Why?

PRIA

I liked the word. It sounded like the exact opposite of the word bucket. Soft. Pretty. Singable.

THEO

I like it.

(joke opera sings) Scintilla!

PRIA

And, okay, I put all those dumb things on it like bungee jumping, sky diving, flying to the moon—

THEO

Meetin' a guy in a hotel room for sex?

PRIA

I was eleven, dude. Bones didn't make the list.

THEO

Singing?

PRIA
Yeah. That was there.

THEO
So let's hear it.

Silence.

Okay, then. I guess . . . we've got nothing left to talk about.
Better get to it . . .

THEO *begins taking his pants off. He stops.*

You know, Pria. You put this all on me . . . it wasn't fair.

Pause.

PRIA
You're right.

THEO
Shit. I didn't mean—I'm sorry. I just mean . . . if you really
believed this was gonna work, you were killing me too.

PRIA
I know.

THEO
So then . . .

PRIA
Are you mad?

THEO
No. I'm not mad.

PRIA
Maybe this is just about sex.

THEO
I don't think that.

    Beat.

PRIA
It was my sister that dated the entire basketball team.

THEO
What?

PRIA
I'm telling you 'cause I think that's really exciting. Not gross.

THEO
All right.

PRIA
She would sneak out.

THEO
Like you're sneaking out.

PRIA
Like I'm sneaking out. Yeah.

And I always knew how important the dude was by the lipstick colour she was wearing. Pink in the Afternoon. That was the one.

With the other guys, she'd just slap on any old sex-bomb red, but with Anthony it was Pink in the Afternoon. And she didn't even need to tell me this. I just knew by watching her get ready. It was special.

And my mom couldn't see it, just like she couldn't see me sneaking out to meet you tonight.

> *Beat.*

So do you like it?

THEO
Like what?

PRIA
(*pouting her lips*) Pink in the Afternoon.

THEO
It's perfect.

PRIA
And I didn't let on that I knew when she was sneaking out. Like Jackie thought because my body is weak, my mind must be weak. You know how that happens? People talk a little slower at us? Little softer . . .

THEO
My friggin' uncle Carlos, yeah.

PRIA
And I heard all the rumours about Jackie, but she should get
to live the way she wants to live with her sick little sister who
hogged all the attention and my mom not noticing her and she
was in control of the whole situation, in control of those dudes.
She was the rope. They were the idiots jumping . . .

I wanted to tell Jackie about tonight. Call her and tell her. But
she might think this is childish. Maybe she'd rat me out. But I
never ratted her out.

Sometimes, I would go into her bedroom and get under the
covers so if my mom came in to check on her, she'd see a body
in the bed and think Jackie was home.

I'd do that for her. Pretend to be her.

And just lay there, hoping I wouldn't cough. That I could hold
it in . . . just . . . long . . . enough . . .

I wonder if she ever came home in the middle of the night after
probably going all the way with Anthony. Felt my warmth still
in her bed. Tasted my sour on her pillow. Privately thanked me
for being so cool. 'Cause she was so cool.

THEO
Cool.

PRIA
I miss being useful to someone, you know.

THEO
I could . . . use you—

PRIA
Dude, stop that sentence right there.

THEO
You know what I mean—

PRIA
Just . . . shhhhhhh . . .

> *She coughs.*
>
> *She stops.*
>
> *He coughs.*
>
> *He stops.*

Okay, cowboy. We're gonna die of old age in here. So I'm gonna sing for you 'cause my sister would've sang for Anthony, and then we're gonna do it.

THEO
You still wanna?

PRIA
Don't you?

THEO
I do.

PRIA
No backing out.

THEO
Pria—

PRIA
And if you laugh, I'll kill you for real.

THEO
Why would I laugh?

PRIA
Just shut up. Okay. I've never done this in front of anyone.
Jumped off the bridge. That means something. Okay?

THEO
What does it mean?

PRIA
What do you think?

SONG 8: THE EXPLOSION ARIA

*PRIA begins to sing. PRIASOPRANO joins, turning the crank
on the music box.*

Soft and silent. You will be there.
Soft and silent. You will be there waiting. Waiting for me.

PRIA & PRIASOPRANO
> Strong and silent, you will be there . . .

PRIA
Waiting.

PRIASOPRANO
> . . . Waiting.
> Here's my secret. You will be there. Waiting for me.
> I know the love of dreams.
> And now I dream with you.
> Forever I dream.
> Ah . . .

THEO kisses PRIA. PRIASOPRANO continues.

Everything escalates between THEO and PRIA.

There is an explosion.

A white crescendo, then black.

Quiet.

When the lights come back up, EAGLEI9 and PRIASOPRANO are in the hotel room. There's a different atmosphere. PRIA and THEO are not there. The music box sits on the bed.

EAGLEI9
What happened?

PRIASOPRANO speaks, doesn't sing.

PRIASOPRANO
Kaboom.

> *PRIASOPRANO is laughing.*

> *EAGLEI9 begins laughing too.*

> *A slow fade on the entire universe as . . .*

COMMENTS CHORUS
What happened, you guys?

Is it safe for us to hook up?

Tell us what happened?

Is it safe? Is it safe? Is it . . . ?

> *A canary flies across the stars.*

> *End.*

SONG 1: VOCAL EXERCISE A

Gareth Williams

Boxed text is spoken over the music.

SONG 2: VOCAL EXERCISE B

Gareth Williams

SONG 3: VOCAL EXERCISE C

Gareth Williams

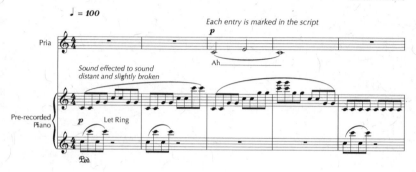

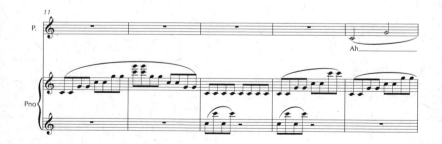

SONG 4: VOCAL EXERCISE D

Gareth Williams

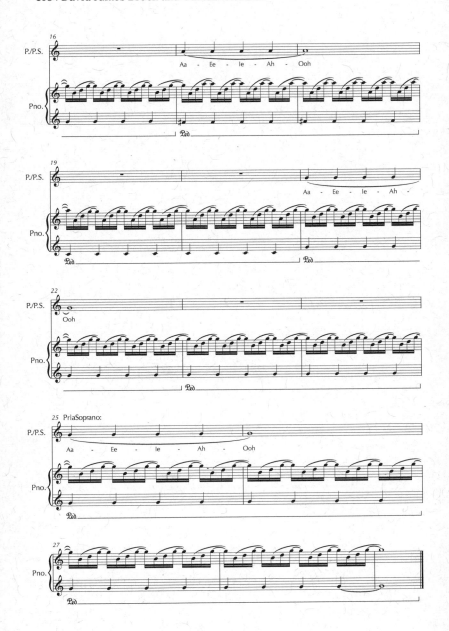

SONG 5: PUNNETT SQUARE MUSIC INTO
LA BOHÈME EXCERPT (ARRANGED BY WILLIAMS)

Arr. Gareth Williams

Piano loops build underneath the scene,
moving to the arrangement of La bohème.

♩ = *100*

Cue to move into song

PriaSoprano: It's ok, Eagle19. I am too.

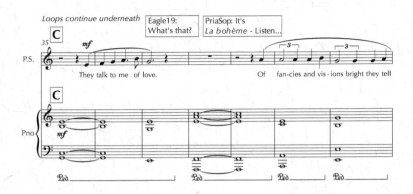

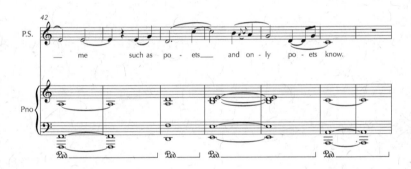

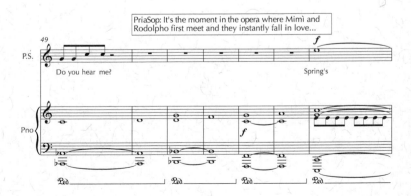

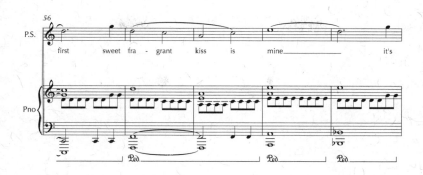

first sweet fra - grant kiss is mine_____ it's

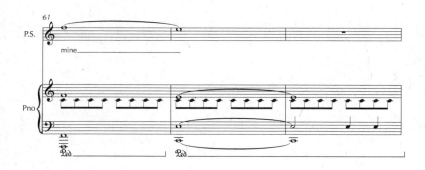

mine_____

Eagle19: I've never done this!   Eagle19: I've never done this!

Can I meet you?   Will you meet me?_

Loops stop with the piano

SONG 6: PRIA'S HOSPITAL SONG

David James Brock

Gareth Williams

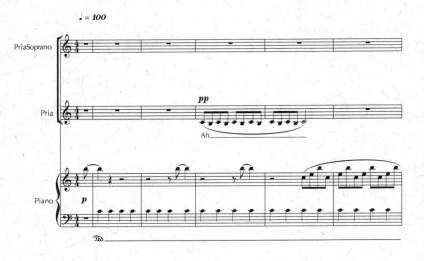

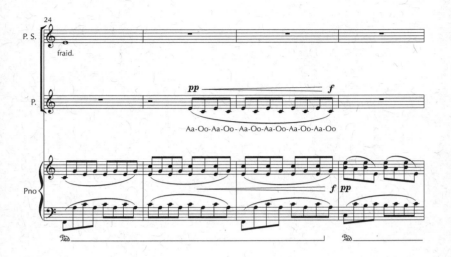

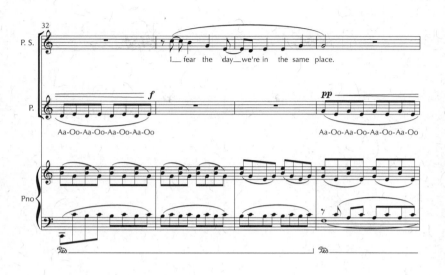

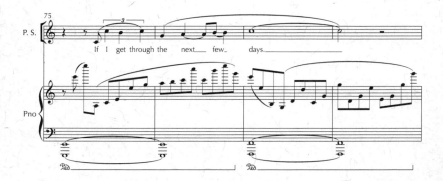

SONG 7: PRIA TAKES US TO THE OPERA

David James Brock

Gareth WIlliams

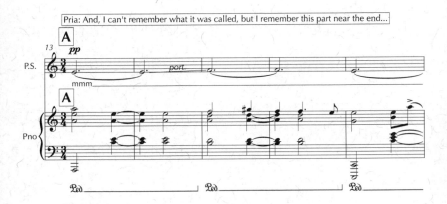

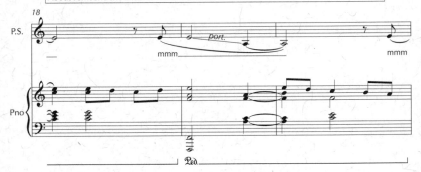

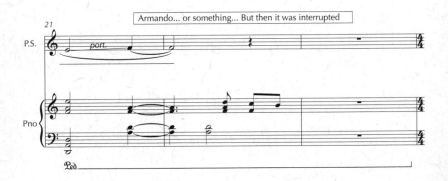

It was her father. He wakes her up and says, **"Today is the day you will marry."**

Theo: Married to the guy she loves in the dream? Armando?

Pria: Of course not, it's opera, dude... She says...

No. No, no, no, no.

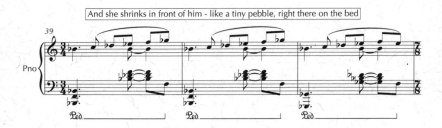

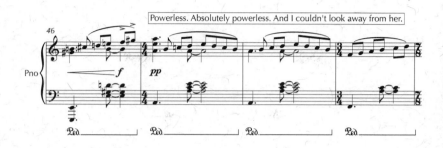

Powerless. Absolutely powerless. And I couldn't look away from her.

Theo: So what happened?

O-kay, O-kay, I will mar-ry him! O-kay, O-kay,

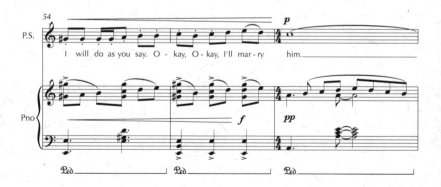

I will do as you say. O-kay, O-kay, I'll mar-ry him.

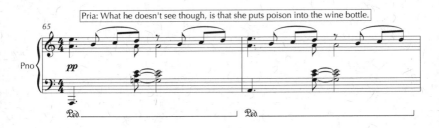

And he says: "**To my daughter on her wedding day! To doing your duty.**
And may you do the next man's bidding better than you did mine."

He takes a gulp! But... then he pours her a glass in return! She pauses for a second...

And then... drains the glass, and smiles.

And her father is happy. He has won.... for the moment. Until...

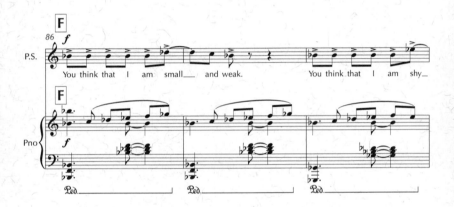

You think that I am small__ and weak. You think that I am shy__

__ and meek. I have known the love of dreams.

I have known the roar of li - ons. I've known the heat of a thou - sand

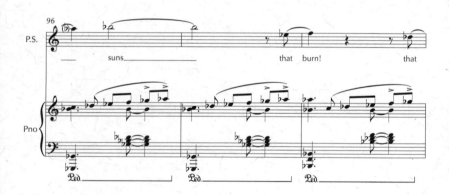

suns that burn! that

burn! that burn while you sleep.

Pria: She starts to feel the poison. She goes back to the bed.

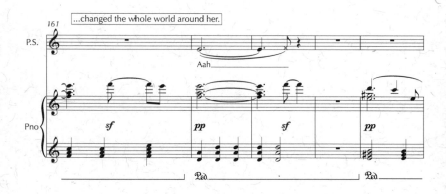

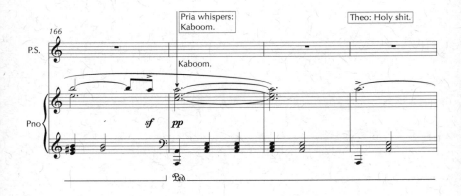

Pria: I went home that night, cried into my pillow. Decided I would take singing lessons.

Theo: And...?

Pria: I'll never sing opera.

SONG 8: THE EXPLOSION ARIA

David James Brock

Gareth Williams

*Pria turns the crank on the music box
and starts to sing very quietly - the sound
of a C Major Arpeggio repeats until
the piano loop takes over.*

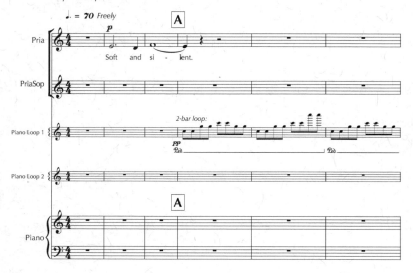

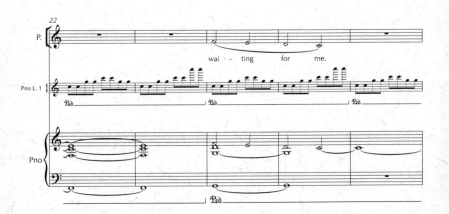

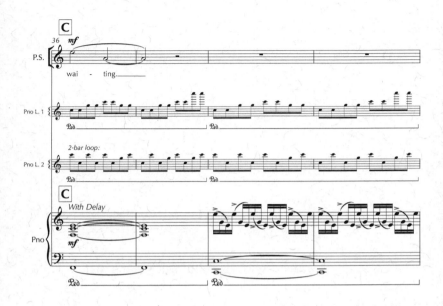

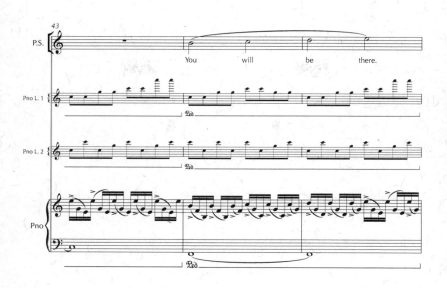

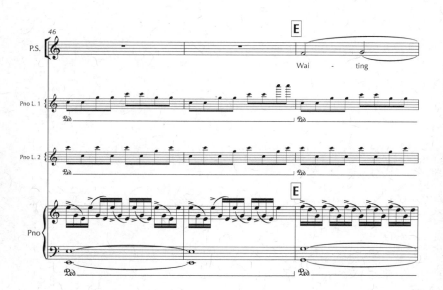

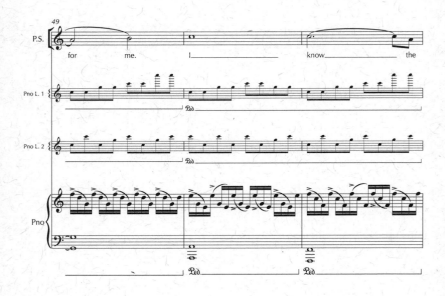

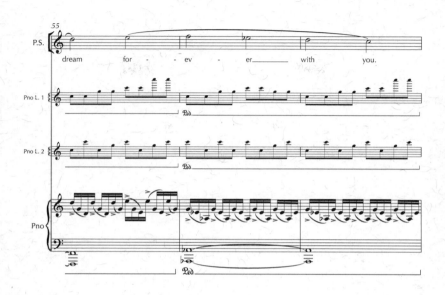

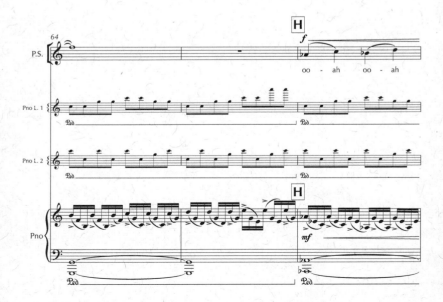

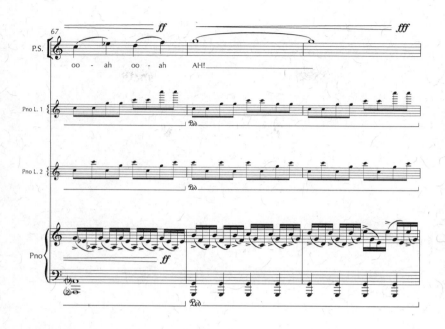

David James Brock is a playwright, poet, librettist, and screen-writer. He is a past winner of the Herman Voaden Canadian National Playwriting Competition for his play *Wet*. Brock is the author of two poetry collections, *Everyone is CO2* and *Ten-Headed Alien* (Wolsak & Wynn). With Scottish Opera, Brock co-created *Breath Cycle*, a multimedia operatic song cycle developed with cystic fibrosis patients. He co-wrote both the opera and screen-play for *Year of the Horse* (with Mike Haliechuk) and the script for the film *Mother of All Shows* (with Melissa D'Agostino). He lives in Toronto.

Northern Irish composer Gareth Williams lives in Edinburgh,
Scotland, where he makes work that seeks to find new participants,
collaborators, and audiences for opera and music theatre to shed
light on stories and communities that have been overlooked, and
to explore ideas of vulnerability in vocal writing. His music is often
site-specific and responsive, with performances happening in light-
houses, whisky distilleries, nuclear bunkers, and libraries. From 2015
to 2018, Williams collaborated with Oliver Emanuel to create the
critically acclaimed 306 Trilogy, a collection of music theatre works
telling the story of the British soldiers shot for cowardice during
WWI, produced by the National Theatre of Scotland. The album
from the trilogy, *Lost Light: Music from the 306*, was released in 2020.
Rocking Horse Winner, produced by Tapestry Opera, was nominated
for nine Dora Mavor Moore Awards in 2017, winning five, includ-
ing Outstanding Musical Production. The opera was recorded and
released in 2020 by Tapestry Opera. Currently, Gareth lectures in
composition at the University of Edinburgh, and is working on new
operas and musicals, as well as a new album as a singer-songwriter.

First edition: March 2022
Printed and bound in Canada by Imprimerie Gauvin, Gatineau

Jacket design by David Gee
Author photo © Anita Nagra

PLAYWRIGHTS
CANADA PRESS

202-269 Richmond St. W.
Toronto, ON
M5V 1X1

416.703.0013
info@playwrightscanada.com
www.playwrightscanada.com
@playcanpress